# Landforms

**Mary Evans**

We can see many different landforms on the Earth. A landform is a natural area that is part of the Earth's surface.

Sawtooth Mountains and Salmon River, Idaho

Hanauma Bay, Hawaii

This landform is called a **bay**. At this place the ocean water pushes into the land. It creates a bay. The edge of this bay looks almost round. People like to come to this bay in Hawaii to swim.

Grand Canyon, Arizona

A **canyon** is a landform made by a river. Over time, the river cuts steep walls into the rock. This is the Grand Canyon. People from all over the world visit the Grand Canyon. It is in Arizona.

Acadia National Park, Maine

This landform is a **cliff**. It is a place where the land drops sharply. A cliff can be by the sea, like this one in Maine.

When there is almost no rain for a very long time, a **desert** is formed. A desert can be hot or cold, but it is always a dry place. This desert in New Mexico is sandy. Nothing grows here.

White Sands desert, New Mexico

These beautiful **hills** are landforms in California. Hills have round tops. They are not as high as mountains.

Cambria, California

Lake Tahoe, California

This landform is an **island**. It has water all around it. You cannot walk on land to an island. You have to swim or go by boat to reach this island in California.

Monument Valley, Arizona

A **mesa** has steep sides and a very flat top.
The word *mesa* is Spanish. It means "table."
The mesa you see here is in Arizona.

**Mountains** are very big landforms. Mountains are taller than hills. They have steep sides. This mountain is Mount Rainier. It is in the state of Washington.

Mount Rainier, Washington

This landform is a **peninsula**. A peninsula has water on three sides. This little peninsula in Massachusetts juts out into the Atlantic Ocean. Some peninsulas are much larger.

Manchester, Massachusetts

Fall River County, South Dakota

This flat, grassy place in South Dakota is a landform called a **plain**. A plain has miles and miles of flat land. It has almost no trees. There are no hills on a plain.

The landform you see here is a **valley**. It is the low place between mountains or hills. This Colorado town is in a valley.

Ouray, Colorado

Mount Saint Helens, Washington

You probably guessed what this landform is. It is a **volcano**. Hot rock from deep inside the Earth is erupting through the top of the volcano. This volcano is Mount Saint Helens. It is in the state of Washington.

# LANDFORMS PICTURE GLOSSARY

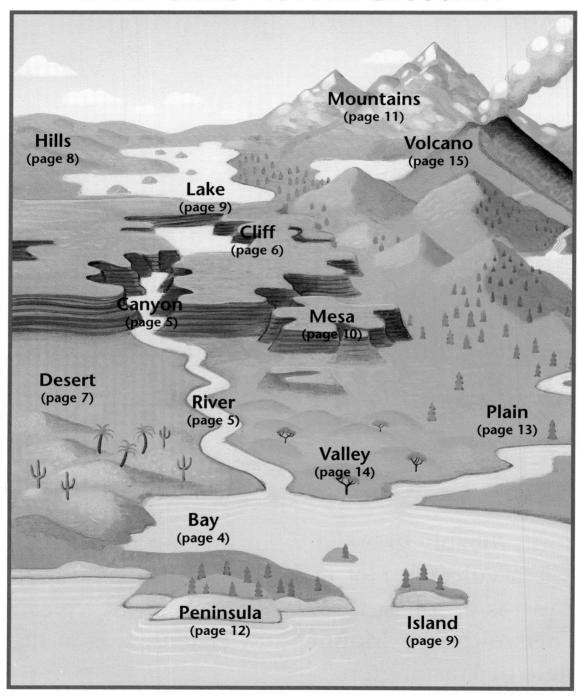

Mountains
(page 11)

Volcano
(page 15)

Hills
(page 8)

Lake
(page 9)

Cliff
(page 6)

Canyon
(page 5)

Mesa
(page 10)

Desert
(page 7)

River
(page 5)

Plain
(page 13)

Valley
(page 14)

Bay
(page 4)

Peninsula
(page 12)

Island
(page 9)